Brazil
Paradise of Gemstones

by Jules Roger Sauer

Photographs by Harold & Erica Van Pelt

1

Acknowledgements

- Professor Jacques P. Cassedanne
  Universidade Federal do Rio de Janeiro

  For his valuable participation in research

- My collaborators, Maria Amélia Silva Pinto, Marina J.G.
  Reis and Daniel A. Sauer for their effort and patience.

PHOTOGRAPHY CREDITS:
Professor Pierre Bariand – Curator of the Mineral Collection
of the University P. et M. Curie (Sorbonne) – Paris
Dr. E. Gübelin, C.F. F.G.A. – Switzerland
Professora Speranza Cavenago-Bignami Moneta – Milan
Erica & Harold Van Pelt – Los Angeles
American Museum of Natural History – New York
De Beers Consolidated Mines
Naturhistorisches Museum – Vienna
Smithsonian Institution – Washington DC

Foreword

For years Brazil has been the major producer of colored stones in the world. Brazilian production has been characterized by a greater variety of gemstones produced than that of any other area. Blessed with a huge pre-Cambrian shield area, cut by thousands of pegmatite dikes and associated metamorphic rocks, the variety of gem deposits in Brazil is almost infinite.

In addition to the mineral assemblage one might expect from pegmatite dikes, Brazil also produces a very significant output of diamonds, as well as fine opals. A recent emerald find is producing magnificent stones.

Until this book was written, there had been no single source of great length and significance devoted specifically to Brazilian gemstones, written in English, and beautifully illustrated.

"Brazil, Paradise of Gemstones", by Jules Roger Sauer, is notable not only for the subject but for the fact that it was written by a man identified for many years with Brazil's gemstones as a prospector, miner, cutter, gem supplier and retailer as well.

Some important discoveries can be attributed to him, such as, aquamarines in Rio Grande do Norte, in 1953, the precious opals of Pedro II in Piauí, in 1960, and a turquoise vein near the village of Casa Nova, in Bahia, later flooded by the waters of the Sobradinho dam. Furthermore, it was due to his personal initiative that the Brazilian emerald was actually recognized by the Gemological Institute of America.

He is best known in the English-speaking world as the proprietor of Amsterdam Sauer, which markets gemstones worldwide, and for his ownership of the Cruzeiro tourmaline and mica mine and the Jacobina amethyst mine. He owns several other mines as well and has a large chain of retail stores, centered in the Rio de Janeiro area, but located in other Brazilian cities as well.

This book is made exceptionally valuable by pictures taken by the famous mineral and gem photographers, Harold and Erica Van Pelt. The magnificent photographs, especially taken of the outstanding collection of Brazilian gemstones assembled over a lifetime by the author, adorn the book and give the reader the opportunity to judge some of the finest of the Brazilian output, particularly of the Twentieth Century.

The book is a showcase of the best from Brazil and it makes a handsome evocation of what is beautiful in gemstones.

Richard T. Liddicoat Jr.
President

Gemological Institute of America

3

Introduction

The search for treasure is a constant strand in the history of mankind. To the impecunious and the free spirit it meant sudden wealth; to the more worldly-wise it was a means of converting a temporary gain into a tangible, lasting asset or else of adding to an existing fortune by investing in something all would recognize as being of great value.

Treasure trove has taken many forms. Cunningly worked swords, rare shells, precious oils and perfumes, have all had their time. Gold and silver utensils made functional objects out of metals prized for their beauty, and valued for their rarity. Treasure might be a mishapen gold nugget or a hunk of rock enclosing a wondrous crystal. Even the untutored, whether simple peasant or pirate freebooter, could not fail to appreciate their possibilities.

But it is the eye and skill of the craftsman which is needed to realize the potential inherent in a lump dug up from the earth's crust. It is he who forms the vital link between the prospector or trader and the customer with taste to appreciate – and pocket to pay – for those luxuries that enhance life and denote success.

Hoarding treasure in the manner of the Ancient World was all very well but what was the use of wealth if it could not be displayed? Man's craving for adornment, to flatter his vanity and fill his pride, is another strand in the skein of this story. Often these adornments would also have symbolic importance or a practical function, showing the wearer's status or forming part of his religious trappings.

Historical references to a primitive form of jewelry go as far back as the Palaeolithic Age, up to three million years ago. More properly described as talismans, these adornments were made of teeth, shells and fossils. The first man who managed to bore a hole through a stone before stringing it to make a necklace was the direct ancestor of the gem-cutter in today's workshops.

Down the centuries the story has varied little in its basic elements. It is one of individual quest, vision to enhance intrinsic beauty and a steady demand for precious stones. Tastes and fashions change.While new discoveries may flood the market one day and the next a productive lode is worked out, paradoxically the erratic supply of precious stones to the retailers has over the years helped to enhance their value.

Diamond prospection expedition during the Empire.

What is it about a clear or coloured rock crystal that makes it valuable? Undoubtedly rarity is the prime characteristic. But if it can also have some practical application, as with diamonds as cutting agents in industry, or strategic purpose, as with quartz crystals in radioelectronics, a further objective dimension is added.

Beauty, on the other hand, is a highly subjective concept. What is dazzling radiance to one man can be dross to the second – and who is to gainsay the latter? In this treacherous field, where natural wonders can be duplicated with synthetic products, experience and reputation become all important.

Rare beauty commands its own price, undictated by any market considerations. Uniqueness of form and colour, drawn out by the cutter's art, ensures a value that will outlive the destruction caused by these inflationary times.

In an age of transience precious stones in their natural state or else transformed into works of art thus assume an even greater importance. The growing awareness of modern man of the finite nature of those riches – a one-time harvest – being dug up at an ever-increasing pace can but confirm the value of what he holds.

Man and earth: the eternal relationship. Suspended between heaven and earth for a brief span of time, man can find in the beauty of a rare diamond or emerald or aquamarine those enduring qualities lacking in himself. The inner fire is not of his making, his role is to glorify the eternal.

In the same manner as Michaelangelo created his immortal David, visualizing him in a block of rough marble, so does the humble gem-cutter discern the radiance of the jewel dormant within the dark and inanimate mineral. His magic worked, the gemstone is freed from its enslaving boundaries.

Little has changed since the days of the Persian empires, of the Pharaohs or the distant Chinese dynasties, in the techniques of this all-embracing vocation: part art, part craft, part commerce. Modern technology, in which computer-controlled design is becoming increasingly common, has virtually no place here. The gem-cutter has merely added electric power to his foot-operated wheel. The skills required remain the same.

Strictly speaking, the term "gemstone" has become the commonly accepted name for all ornamental stones of value, eliminating the previous artificial distinction between so-called "precious" and "semi-precious" stones.

With the growing appreciation over the past 30 years of the wide variety of stones previously denigrated as being only "semi-precious" – tourmaline, aquamarine, agate and amethyst, for example – the distinction between the two categories has become obsolete. In many cases the latter now fetch higher prices than traditionally more desired stones.

Diamond mining in the state of Bahia, during the Empire.

Freed from traditional considerations, the recognition of the beauty of coloured stones such as those which Brazil possesses in abundance, has placed the industry on a more rational basis. It is yet one more example of the way in which present generations have been able to benefit by freeing themselves of the blinkers of the past, in which conformity to previously set norms was prescribed.

One outstanding feature which sets the world of gemstones apart from almost any other field is its individualism. Without the individual prospector, the master cutter and the entrepreneur with vision and faith, the industry could never have reached its present heights.

In Brazil, much credit must go to the "bandeirantes" and especially the "garimpeiros", the country's original pioneers and the mineral prospectors who came in their wake. Pushing into an unknown interior populated by often hostile Indian tribes, Brazil's pioneers chanced across many of the finds still being worked today.

From the gateways of Salvador in the North-East of Bahia state, and from Rio and São Paulo further South, the pioneers made their way to the Jequitinhonha Valley and the Mantiqueira mountain range in today's Minas Gerais state. The rich mineral deposits these early eighteenth century explorers found there were enshrined in the new state's name: "General Mines".

While mining companies quickly established themselves in Minas Gerais to use their capital and trading knowledge to exploit the large deposits of base and precious minerals, there was also a place for the fortune seeker panning the region's many rivers.

After its discovery by the Portuguese in 1500, Brazil's early history was shaped in large part by the search for gold and precious stones. In 1728 the first diamonds found by gold panners in the streams of Minas Gerais reached Lisbon, the colonial capital. Prospectors rushed to search the waters of this hilly state resting on a Pre-Cambrian shield. They were not disappointed.

For nearly a century and a half, Brazil was the world's leading diamond producer, taking over from India whose mines were near depletion. Slave labour, as on the plantations, was a key to success.

The colonial link between Brazil and Goa, on India's south-west coast, proved a profitable one for the first dealers in Brazilian diamonds. They were able to trade on the established reputation of Indian stones to sell their own finds through Goa to the European market.

As Brazil had eclipsed India, so a new colonial upstart, South Africa, in turn put Brazil in the shade, around 1866. Brazil remains a significant producer of diamonds, from relatively small deposits scattered around the country. But statistics are hard to obtain in view of that individualism, which prompted the search in the first place.

Minas Gerais and the Mato Grosso region, in the center of the country, are still the most important producing areas. But other commercial deposits are also found in the states of Goiás, Bahia, São Paulo, Maranhão, Pará and Piauí.

Open pit emerald mining in Santa Terezinha de Goiás, state of Goiás, 1981.

9

With its eight and a half million square kilometres – bigger than continental United States – and its ancient ore-bearing rock, Brazil is undoubtedly one of the earth's last great reserves of mineral wealth. Moreover, much of its area has still to be surveyed properly. Even so the range and richness of the gemstones already discovered gives it fair claim to being the world's leading producer of coloured stones.

Its rise to preeminence is associated with the rise in value of the coloured stones it has in abundance but which attracted little attention in the local or world market until the Second World War.

As in many other fields of fashion and culture, for decades the dominant influence in Brazil had been Europe. In Brazil, until 1940, local stones of outstanding beauty were neglected in favour of synthetic rubies or sapphires. The "dependence mentality" so debilitating to the growth of a domestic industry in its own right permitted Brazil to remain for the first half of this century as a supplier of relatively low-priced, albeit splendid stones to the world market.

It took the world conflict, into which Brazil was sucked, to create international interest in Brazilian gems. Ironically, though, it was quartz and mica, the settings within which today's most popular gems are found, which were the object of the new wave of prospecting – and not the coloured stones themselves.

The crystals had assumed an unexpected additional dimension, as they were needed in piezoelectronics for use in radio transmission, sonar equipment and aircraft frequency control. Demand rocketed as the Allied powers scrambled to secure their supplies, of which Brazil was the most bountiful source.

It was against this background that new pioneers in Brazil, among them the author, saw the benefits for the country of establishing an indigenous gem-cutting industry.

In 1941, the author had established his own workshop in Belo Horizonte, capital of Minas Gerais state, within a short distance of the country's main gem-producing areas. The city lacked a tradition of skilled workers capable of handling the delicate work of this trade. Turning adversity to advantage the author maintained, however, that a shoeshine boy could easily learn to polish stones under expert guidance. Few of his hundred workers had had any previous professional experience.

The appearance in the early post-war years of a new, free form of cutting and mounting local stones was perhaps the most important development of all for the embryonic Brazilian gemstone industry. Instead of splitting large stones into small, insignificant pieces suitable for traditional European mountings, more appropriate for specimens of lesser size, the new Brazilian school of cutters preserved their reverence for the shape and dimension of the material they were dealing with, no longer inhibited by the sclerotic classical patterns imposed from across the ocean.

Goldsmith workshops of the same school sprang up alongside. Master jewellers who had fled the conflict or else sought new opportunities in Brazil during the austere post-war years in Europe formed the foundation stone of today's flourishing industry. Initially they were

Manual excavation to detect the emerald layer, Goiás, 1981.

responding to the demand from clients cut off from their previous suppliers by the ravages of the war in Europe. A prominent figure in this adventurous new phase was the well known Belgian Henrique Wijstraat, the overseer of the author's workshop.

Meanwhile the much higher prices Brazilian minerals were fetching prompted renewed prospecting thoughout the country. The finest examples of quartz and mica are found in pegmatites – coarse-grained intrusions of rock within finer beds – and the associated coloured stones were a lucky bonus. New finds were made in Minas Gerais as well as in non-traditional gem states such as Paraíba, Rio Grande do Norte and Ceará in the Northeast. Furthermore, the founding of Brasilia opened up a new El Dorado to prospectors: the hitherto isolated, wild interior of Goiás state.

Topaz, tourmaline and aquamarine, to quote but a few, were gemstones which over the next 30 years were to see their value soar impressively, far in excess of other varieties or, indeed, inflation.

Brazil is notable for being the only commercial producer in the world of the most valuable form of topaz, the "imperial" variety, mined on the outskirts of the historic city of Ouro Preto, the former capital of Minas Gerais state, and in the surrounding area. Gems of extraordinary beauty in colours ranging from yellow through sherry to delicate pinks are extracted. In 1970, blue topazes of exceptional purity and perfect form were discovered, in the Jequitinhonha region in the north of the state.

Aquamarines too have capitalized in recent years on the quality of Brazilian specimens. An early find, in 1910, weighed in at more than a hundred kilogrammes, a phenomenal weight. The colossal Marambaya aquamarine crystal, as it is known, would today be worth over US$ 25 million. At the time it was of little more than curiosity value.

A foremost example of Brazil's mineral wealth is certainly the tourmaline, the most exciting of all gemstones, present in its baffling variety of colours and hues, which can be counted in the million. Production from the Cruzeiro mine, in Minas Gerais, is famous the world over. A promising future awaits this gem as a modern alternative for the largely exhausted stocks of traditionally more valued stones, emerald, sapphire and ruby. Brazilian tourmaline can match their beauty in some of its different varieties: "cromolite" (green), indicolite (blue) and rubellite (red).

Notwithstanding the appreciation belatedly given to these formerly "semi-precious" stones, it was only in 1963, with the discovery of emeralds in commercial quantities and quality that Brazil could finally be said to have confirmed its world preeminence as a gemstone producer. Doubtless, the age-old, universal acceptance of the fabled stone consolidated Brazil's position, acting as a beachhead for its immense variety of other mineral treasures. Now, emerald accounts for half the revenue of the country's gemstone industry and most of the prospection endeavours now in process.

The story of Brazilian emeralds on the world market follows the same course as in early epochs was enacted first with diamonds and later with other of the country's gemstones: initial neglect, indeed disdain, followed by grudging acceptance of their intrinsic fine quality, and finally realization of their full value on their own merits.

Gold digging in Serra Pelada, state of Pará, 1980.

Credit must be given in this respect to an elite clientèle of international residents, who proved largely responsible for the recognition of Brazilian gemstones abroad. The Brazilian public, with the exception of a few distinguished collectors, failed for some time to acknowledge their beauty and uniqueness.

Nothing breeds success better than success itself. Sometimes it is luck which gives the initial break, sometimes historical circumstances, sometimes an act of faith to create a market where none existed beforehand. Whatever the route, it is a fact that the mushrooming of the Brazilian gemstone industry, now fully integrated from extraction to retailing, is the long overdue realization of its potential.

The discovery and marketing of the emeralds is one such example. Found in Salininha in the state of Bahia, these exceptional transparent and often double-terminated crystals were initially difficult to sell. The author therefore submitted samples, in 1963, to the Gemological Institute of America to obtain authoritative testimony to their nature. They were confirmed as gem quality emeralds.

While many starved, sometimes only a few feet away from fantastic finds, fortunes have been made overnight by private prospectors in locations such as Carnaíba in Bahia state and, more recently, in Santa Terezinha de Goiás in Goiás state. The role of the garimpeiro cannot be underestimated in finding emeralds and other gems.

However, the possibility of mechanizing the production process vastly enhances commercial possibilities. So far this is relatively uncommon in Brazil. None the less, an emerald occurrence – in Itabira, north of Belo Horizonte – has proved capable of mechanization. Discovered only in 1979, this process is now underway.

In one generation Brazil has established a gemstone industry unequalled in the southern hemisphere in its full complement of skills. This encompasses mining, cutting, polishing, setting, marketing and exporting. Whereas in 1940 perhaps only a dozen retail outlets existed, today there are over 500 registered firms. Half a million people are employed in the prospection and transformation of gemstones, or related activities. A small town in the interior of Minas Gerais, Teofilo Otoni alone numbers around 14,000 garimpeiros among its population.

Paralleling the development of many of Brazil's other raw material industries which have progressed from being mere suppliers to the world to a fully integrated status, the gemstone business has now reached maturity. Furthermore, because of the important place it has carved for itself in the world trade, Brazil has attained the privileged position where it is its own traders and brokers who set, to a certain extent, the market quotations in coloured gemstones, following no fixed guidelines apart from cost plus marginal profit. High stocks maintained by Brazilian dealers are another muscular reason why it is able to compete effectively with other countries where production fluctuates more wildly.

Establishing an amazing example, Brazil has soared after 40 years of steady growth to an enviously strong situation in the world's gemstone industry.

*"Gemstones
a one-time harvest."*
Jules Roger Sauer

Photographs from De Beers.

Diamond

Although this book focuses on coloured gemstones, it would be incomplete without a chapter on diamond. This was the first stone to be commercially exploited in Brazil, and was decisive in putting the country on the world's mineral map.

Between 1725 and 1866, Brazil was the world's foremost producer before being eclipsed by South Africa. After nearly a century in the shade, it is once again beginning to recover lost ground. Unlike some other former producing countries, such as India, where diamond mines are almost worked out, there is firm evidence that the Brazilian product is far from exhaustion.

Famous diamonds found in Brazil are the President Vargas, with 726 carats, the Darcy Vargas, with 460 carats, and the President Dutra, with 342 carats.

Today several thousand garimpeiros are engaged in diamond mining on sites scattered over a 4,000 kilometre area, from the Rio Branco plateau on the Venezuelan border to the north of Minas Gerais and Mato Grosso do Sul state. Many of the producing regions are sparsely populated and have been only cursorily prospected.

Since before the days of the Brazilian Empire, from the early 18th to the late 19th century, diamonds have been worked around a town on the Jequitinhonha river in Minas Gerais which came to be called Diamantina. However, it is the Estrela do Sul region in the extreme west of the state that has produced the country's largest specimens. The proximity of kimberlites, absent on the Jequitinhonha, could in future lead prospectors to the discovery of productive intrusive rocks.

Geologically, these two producing areas come from quite different periods. While those in the Estrela do Sul date back to between 120 and 150 million years, those in the Diamantina region have probably existed for 500 to a billion years.

In Brazil, although more than 300 kimberlites have been found, none has provided a viable diamond yield. Mining has therefore always taken place in alluvium, eluvium and ancient agglomerates. Mechanization is hindered by an incomplete knowledge of deposit configuration. The only location where mechanization has been possible is at Tejucana, on the Jequitinhonha.

The diamond deposits in Mato Grosso and Goiás states have never been the object of major surveys.

Canary-yellow diamond.

Beryls

Emerald

The peerless emerald. Without its chance discovery, Brazil would never have fulfilled its aspirations to be in the first rank of the world's leading coloured gemstone producers.

With its unique deep green colour, in ancient times the emerald was held to be a symbol of imortality and faith. It has always possessed a certain mystique, perhaps because of the way in which it seems to pull one's eye deep inside itself, to unfathomable depths. At the same time its consistently high value has made it a status symbol par excellence.

Four countries alone are still productive: Zambia and Zimbabwe in Africa and Colombia and Brazil in South America. Of these, Brazil today appears to be the most stable supplier in view of its geopolitical position.

The first commercial emerald occurrence was discovered in Salininha, near Pilão do Arcado, Bahia state, in 1963. Other occurrences had been previously noted in such locations as Anagé, Brumado, Ituaçu and Porto – all in the state of Bahia – but did not prove viable. In Minas Gerais state, emeralds were found in Araçuaí, Guanhães, João Pinheiro, Sabinópolis, São José de Corutuba (Grão Mogol), Juerana and Santana dos Ferros, but were not exploited.

Group of emeralds from mines in the states of Bahia (Salininha and Carnaíba) and Minas Gerais (Itabira).

Double-terminated emerald crystal, eight centimetres long, incrusted in quartz (Carnaíba mine, state of Bahia).

The Salininha deposit is an east-west lenticular pegmatite, sandwiched between gneiss and carbonated talc schists. The colour of the stones is probably due to the presence of vanadium, associated with the basic rock in the vicinity. (Note: this metal is abundantly found in the great iron and titanium reserves presently being surveyed in neighbouring Campo Alegre de Lourdes).

Prospection was later carried out in the Fazenda das Lajes, 34 kilometres southeast of the city of Goiás, in Goiás state. Emeralds were scattered in the clay and residual gravel covering the lower slopes of the Dourada mountain range. Associated minerals are magnetite, ilmenite, rutile, quartz, talc, actinolite, tourmaline, chlorite and microcline.

The Jacobina range, which stretches for 150 kilometres along a north to south axis in Bahia, revealed a whole string of emerald occurrences in 1965. The area had been known since 1921 as producer of amethyst. Most notable was the famous Coxo mine, near the town of Jacobina. The emerald discoveries, concentrated in the Pindobaçu municipality, 30 kilometres south of Campo Formoso, are considered to be the most important deposits to have been found to date in Brazil. The deposits are globally known as Carnaíba.

The geological context is a mid-pre-Cambrian north-south trend, composed mainly of quartzitic rock, surrounded everywhere by more ancient gneiss. Ultrabasic rock intruded on the west side of the range, where chromite mines are worked. The emerald deposits occupy the same structural position as the chromite, around a large granite batholith. The latter forms a series of pegmatite veins of one to two metres width, made up of oligoclase – often kaolinized – muscovite and beryl. Quartz veins sprout from them with beryl, schorl and biotite, in the

Jewels set with emeralds from the Carnaíba and Itabira mines.

ultrabasic rock as well as in the quartzite encasing them. In contact with the pegmatites, a micaceous rock with a thickness varying from one to two metres, known as sludite, can be observed.

This rock is essentially composed of mica, intermediate between biotite and phlogopite, arranged in parallel scales. Hence the frequently-used name of biotiteschist. Emerald is scattered in the sludite or lies in aggregates associated with quartz, molybdenite, apatite, schorl, black mica and scheelite specks. The occurrence is classified as a migmatite pegmatite of hybrid origin. It is intrusive in the ultrabasic rock of the penultimate Tectonic phase which marked the emergence of the Jacobina range.

The emerald crystals reach a few centimetres in diametre, with an intense, greasy, vitreous lustre, rarely transparent, but always of a lovely green, much desired by cutters and collectors.

Mining in Carnaíba is presently undergoing difficulties and production is declining. Almost all the vertical shafts have reached a depth of 150 metres; water is continuously infiltrating the work front, forcing the garimpeiros into an endless pumping ordeal.

Work is less complicated in the Marota occurrence, six kilometres from the Jacobina mountains. Here, open-pit mining is often possible. Emerald crystals from this mine are mostly large, sometimes attaining 500 carats. The colour, however, is less intense than those produced uphill, and is restricted in many cases to the crystal's surface.

Other emerald occurrences certainly exist in the Jacobina range, because of the proximity of the Campo Formoso chromium mine. Locating such deposits cannot always be done in a methodical manner. The outcrops which give a geologist the best clues for potential prospection are often covered by soil and thus difficult to interpret. Furthermore, land-owners fear invasions by garimpeiros and prefer to conceal tell-tale signs of an occurrence. They do so despite the fact that Brazilian law guarantees them a stake in the discovery of underground wealth.

The Itabira municipality, in Minas Gerais state, has long been known for its pegmatites. Here an important emerald occurrence was located, practically on the surface, in 1979. The crystals are characterized by microscopic needles paralled to the hexagonal prisms. The green has a splendid hue, slightly yellow, strongly dichroic, sometimes of the most desired quality. This locality is being mechanized at present and large-scale production is foreseen in the near future.

The most recent discovery dates from April 1981. It occurred 24 kilometres from the town of Santa Terezinha de Goiás, in Goiás state. The emeralds are mined in open pits from a matrix of decomposed talc schist. Work accomplished to date seems to indicate a promising occurrence. Other outcrops nearby open the possibility of a vast emerald-producing region of which the limits are still unknown.

Fifty four carat emerald, mounted into a diamond necklace (Carnaíba mine, state of Bahia).

Aquamarine

Aquamarine is certainly still the best-known Brazilian gemstone. Its colours range throughout the spectrum of blue, reflecting all the shades found in the seas along Brazil's immense Atlantic coastline. Today, it has to share the limelight with the recently discovered emerald finds. Nevertheless its own value has risen at a faster rate than almost any other gemstone, especially for its rarer, more subtle specimens. However, judging value can be extremely tricky because of the fact that barely perceptible changes in colour have a disproportionately great impact on the gem's rarity – and therefore price. At the top end of the scale, value can only be judged by experts with daily experience in the market place.

For almost a century, aquamarines have been found here which are incomparably superior in size, beauty and colour to those of any other source of production.

In 1910 a single aquamarine crystal, which produced a staggering 550,000 carats, was found in the Marambaia region in Minas Gerais state. This crystal, in terms of dimension alone, holds the world record in gem aquamarines. A second famous specimen, found in 1954, weighed 35 kilogrammes and is the most valuable to have been discovered in the world.

Countless others of lesser dimensions, but mostly of great beauty, have made Brazil the country for aquamarines.

A famous gemologist, writing on beryls, states that aquamarines are the "poor cousins" of emeralds. Better would be to say that they are "sisters" since they are chemically identical. Granted, no knowledge exists of emerald crystals in dimensions comparable to the two mentioned specimens. But from a purely aesthetic point of view, one is a blue and the other a green beryl.

Aquamarines made Teófilo Otoni, justifiably, the country's gemstone capital. Nearly all the production has always taken place within a hundred-kilometre radius of this city. The Mucuri region is particularly significant. Prospecting and mining activities in the area have now dwindled, due to the fact that many farmers have preferred to invest in coffee plantations.

Deposits of note in Minas Gerais are in Pedra Azul (formerly called Fortaleza), Medina, Agua Vermelha, Três Barras, Marambaia, Coronel Murta, Itambacuri, Ariranha, Juerana, Araçuaí, Atalaia, Bom Jardim do Trevo, Boqueirão, Brejo, Capelinha, Carangola, Conceição do Serro, Conselheiro Pena, Espera Feliz, Galiléia, Salinópolis, Santa Maria do Suaçuí, Santana dos Ferros, São José de Brejaúba, São Miguel do Jequitinhonha and Rio Mucuri. Other states have important deposits, namely:
- Alagoas: Traipu;
- Ceará: the Solonópole region, Coité, Quixadá and Tauá;
- Espírito Santo: Itaguaçu, Rio Novo (Rodeio) and Pau Grande;
- Paraíba: the Tenente Ananias region;
- Rio Grande do Norte: Caicó, Carnaúbas, Martins, Pau de Ferros, Acari, Alexandria, Equador, Parelhas and São Tomé. The last named is where the first important discovery took place in 1953.

Other beryls associated with the aquamarine are morganite, heliodor and "chartreuse" beryl.

The greenish-blue colour of aquamarine is due to iron traces. The optic axis always shows a greener tone, whereas the blue becomes prominent perpendicular to this axis. Dichroism is more apparent in deeper colours.

Aquamarine is a typical pegmatite mineral. Industrial beryl found in pegmatites is an important mineral for iron alloys, but only a small fraction of pegmatites yields gem quality.

In primary deposits, aquamarine is always close to the quartz core, or wrapped in the surrounding feldspathic masses.

Associated minerals, aside from quartz, feldspar and mica common to all deposits, vary according to their location. The main ones are: cassiterite, columbotantalite, rutile, monazite, zircon, rare earth niobotantalates, apatite, sometimes bismuth and bismuthinite, and, sporadically, iron and manganese phosphates. Their presence as dark masses with coloured cavities, indicate a zone rich in industrial and, sometimes, gem minerals. Among these phosphates, the most frequent are barbosalite, frondelite, hureaulite, heterosite, purpurite, scorzalite, strengite and tavorite.

Aquamarines from the Coronel Murta mine, state of Minas Gerais, mounted in a diamond necklace.

Marquise-cut aquamarine ring (Medina mine, state of Minas Gerais.)

Amblygonite, spodumene and lepidolite are often observed, as well as tourmaline. However, aquamarine -yielding pegmatites occur in fields poor to sterile in quality tourmalines.

Kaolinized pegmatites – those where the feldspars have decomposed – are the most sought after, because of the ease with which the crystals can be separated from their clayish gangue.

Eluvial deposits can be identified by reddish sediments contrasting with those of pegmatite deposits, which are always clear, snowy or off-white. Stones very often show signs of erosion and cracks invaded by argilaceous, reddish limonite.

In alluvium, aquamarines are frequently accompanied by other gemstones, mainly tourmalines and topazes. In certain regions, one gemstone predominantes over others.

"Aquamarine weighing 5,875 grammes, from Marambaia, state of Minas Gerais, acquired in 1911 by J.P. Morgan – Property of the Natural History Museum – New York".

Group of mounted and loose aquamarines, all of superlative quality. The brooch stone weighs 54 carats and was cut from a 35 - kilogramme crystal, the famous "Marta Rocha" aquamarine. The pair of drop earrings come from Itaguaçu, state of Espírito Santo. The ring stone is from Medina and the five loose aquamarines from other localities in the state of Minas Gerais.

Other beryls

Morganite

Pink beryl owes its particularly attractive colour to the presence of manganese and iron.

Main deposits, all in Minas Gerais state, are: Sapucaia (Galiléia municipality), associated with rose quartz and heliodor, Barra de Salinas, Calisto, Jequitinhonha and Minas Novas. Another deposit lies in Equador, in Rio Grande do Norte state.

The main discovery was made at the beginning of 1970 in Córrego do Urucum, in Minas Gerais. An immense geode was coated with kunzite and morganite crystals, the latter weighing more than ten kilogrammes apiece.

Large morganite, from the Sapu-caia mine, state of Minas Gerais. – Property of the Naturhistorisches Museum of Vienna .

Beryl from Juerana, state of Minas Gerais.

Heliodor

A yellow beryl, heliodor owes its colour to the presence of iron with traces of manganese and titanium. It is found in Bom Jesus do Lufa, Dois de Abril, Guanhães, Joaima, Minas Novas, Sabinópolis, Serro and Sapucaia, in Minas Gerais state.

The green to greenish-yellow beryl owes its colour to iron. It is common to pegmatite deposits and sometimes associated with aquamarine.

Blue beryl, of the "cat's eye" variety, from Bom Jesus Itabapoana, state of Espírito Santo.

"Beryl/morganite, measuring 25 centimetres, from Córrego do Urucum, state of Minas Gerais — reproduced from 'Le Monde Merveilleux des Mineraux', by P. Bariand (Curator of Mineral Collection of Sorbonne University Paris)".

Tourmalines

Tourmaline

At the beginning of the 18th century, when the country's pioneers penetrated the forests of Minas Gerais looking for emeralds – only to unwittingly find tourmalines – they felt certain that they had discovered the object of their quest. To this day, green tourmaline is still sometimes erroneously called "Brazilian emerald".

But then tourmaline has always confused the layman; its endless variety of colours and hues can cause it to be mistaken for any other stone. Isomorphic replacement explains this riot of colour, which can vary from one extremity to another within a single crystal, causing a pleochromatic effect. Apart from green, the following varieties are generally recognized: achroite, colourless; rubellite, pink to red; indicolite, blue; siberite, violet; and schorl, black. Green comes in a wide variety of hues, of which the chrome-rich variety known as "cromolite" is particularly notable.

Brazil is the world's main source of tourmaline, a privileged position now that this stone has acquired heightened status as an alternative in its own right for the more classical stones in increasingly limited supply.

Bicoloured tourmalines from the Cruzeiro mine, state of Minas Gerais.

Watermelon tourmaline (note pink centre) on a translucent lepidolite matrix.

Large polychromatic crystal of green-pink elbaite, Cruzeiro mine, state of Minas Gerais. Length: 26 centimetres.

The variety of chrome tourmaline —"cromolite"— deserves special mention for its hue. Only a small proportion of fine medium-dark green tourmalines are transparent when observed along the optic axis. Resemblance to the emerald has made cromolite incomparable as an alternative. At a time when high-quality synthetic emerald fetches several hundred dollars per carat, the reasons why fine cromolite has become one of the most desired gemstones are obvious.

Blue tourmaline — indicolite — is not found in commercial quantities and has become mainly a collectors item. The gemstone's resemblance to sapphire makes it an excellent alternative.

It is the characteristics of the rough material which determine the tourmaline's cut, more than with any other stone. The more transparent, inclusion-free specimens are fashioned mostly into emerald cut, with the table parallel to the axis of the crystal, always intensely pleochroic. Other types of faceted shapes are: oval, round, marquise, pear and some fancy shapes. The cabochon cut is preferred when minute parallel fibrous like inclusions are present, which create the chatoyant variety known as cat's eye. The "watermelon" tourmaline, whose concentric colours changes from red at the crystal's centre to green in the outer layers is cut into slices perpendicular to the principal axis. The sections are transparent or translucent according to the inner purity of the rough stone. Such a cut enhances the marvelous colour compositions and is much in demand in the jewelry market.

Fashioned tourmalines of the so-called "cromolite" variety.

Tourmalines are mainly found in pegmatites and the gem bearing gravel deriving from them. Primary deposits are pegmatites of the zoned (heterogeneous) type. From the wall rock towards the core, various roughly parallel zones can be observed:

– in contact with the wall rock, a narrow strip rich in tiny, needle-shape tourmaline crystals or even sometimes tourmalinite itself. It is improbable to find any gem crystals in this strip of black or very dark stones;
– a micaceous zone, with quartz and feldspar;
– a zone rich in feldspar with quartz and a little beryl, where geodes can occasionally be coated with gem tourmalines;
– a narrow zone, in contact with the core, containing beryl, iron and manganese phosphates, or industrial minerals (columbotantalite, cassiterite, rare earth minerals) and tourmalines:
– finally the core, either single or multiple, is of massive quartz. Some crystals point outwards, on rare occasions of a pink colour. The two zones closest to the core can be rich in lepidolite.

View of the Cruzeiro mine (state of Minas Gerais) considered one of the largest tourmaline mines in the world.

Splendid specimen of several tourmaline crystals terminated by a wide basal plane (Cruzeiro mine, Minas Gerais, found in 1971). Weight: 8,400 grammes.

A number of states (Bahia, Ceará, Espírito Santo, Goiás, Paraíba and Rio de Janeiro) all produce tourmaline. However, the most substantial production comes from the state of Minas Gerais, where a well-known tourmaline basin is centered on the 17th line of latitude south and the 42nd line of longitude west. The basin is delineated to the north by the Jequitinhonha river, to the west by the Araçuaí river (a tributary of the former), on the southwestern side by the Mucurí river and on its eastern side by the Aimorés mountain range. Tourmaline-rich pegmatites, frequently decomposed, are countless.

Tourmaline partially enclosed by cleavelandite, with a quartz crystal on top.

Exceptional tourmaline crystal enclosed by cleavelandite. Measures 26 centimetres. The crystal's inner colour is translucent green, as can be observed at the upper right of the picture.

The main deposits are in the following areas:

Salinas and the Salinas river (Porteira, Boqueirão, Lagoa do Alto) producing pink and green tourmalines;

The Araçuaí-Itinga region and Piauí river (Pirineus mine), famous for their green and blue tourmalines;

The Itamarandiba, Malacacheta and Minas Novas region, boasting exquisite green stones;

Northeast of Teófilo Otoni at Marambaya and Ladinha, where garimpeiros dig up fabulous green, pink and watermelon tourmalines.

The famous Cruzeiro deposit, known the world over for its intense, pigeon-blood rubellites.

A magnificent tourmaline cluster with parallel crystals. The colour changes gradually from green to pink (Santa Rosa deposit, state of Minas Gerais, sound in 1965). Weight: 5,800 grammes. (right)

Indicolite, pinkish-purple tourmaline, verdelite.

Rubellite

Rubellite is the most precious variety of the tourmaline species. Just as the diamond is most valuable when red, and the ruby most desired when pigeon-blood, so is the red tourmaline – or rubellite – the most prized variety... and a choice alternative for ruby. Crystal colour ranges from pale-rose to pigeon-blood, and the percentage of pure rubellite is minute. The illustrations in this book show that only very few rubellite crystals are devoid of visible inclusions. But inclusions in rubellites have become as accepted in jewelery as "gardens" in emeralds. Other natural alternatives for ruby would be spinel and pyrope. However, in Brazil red spinel only comes in minute crystals, while pyrope, when large, displays too dark a hue to resemble ruby.

Mounted rubellite, pigeon-blood colour.

Various colours of tourmaline, resulting from isomorphic replacements. Iron (with magnesium) produces a dark blue, greenish blue or black gemstone; magnesium the achroite, or the yellow-brown and yellowish varieties: chrome a tourmaline resembling emerald: sodium, lithium and potassium produce achroites and green, pink, red and brownish gemstones: manganese colourless to pink gemstones, and, when mixed with iron, blue or green specimens. (left)

In 1977, a small lithium pegmatite was unearthed near Conselheiro Pena, on the banks of the Doce river. It contained a geode filled with cleavelandite and pink to pigeon-blood rubellite crystals, to this day the largest ever found in the world. All the crystals are collectors' specimens. Any collection worthy of the name should include at least one specimen of this century's exceptional treasure. The photographs in this book illustrate this impressive discovery better than words.

Rubellite jewels, showing that certain tourmalines resemble the pigeon-blood ruby, from the Cruzeiro mine, state of Minas Gerais.

Rubellite crystal, double-terminated, inclusion-free, studded with delicate cleavelandite rosettes.

The "Pair of Shoes". The two diagonal ends "exploded" and continued to grow. When the prisms are joined together they fit perfectly into each other. Length: 38 centimetres.

Partial view of a giant agglomerate weighing 164 kilogrammes composed of fine terminated rubellites and quartzes, in a cleavelandite matrix. (Conselheiro Pena − Minas Gerais − 1977).

50

No museum or collection possesses a complete spectrum of tourmalines.Each new crystal presents such unique characteristics that it can differ totally from another tourmaline encountered a few inches away within the same pegmatitic body. Drastic colour variations can occur within the same crystal. The hues of this gemstone are so numerous that many collectors specialize exclusively in tourmalines.

Terminated rubellite crystals forming one sole pyramid. Height: 35 centimetres. (right)

Brooch and necklace set with fine rubellites.

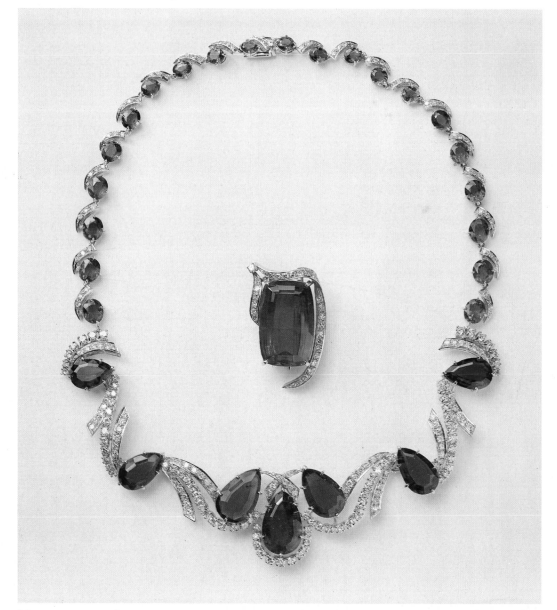

Topaz

Group of imperial topaz in various hues from pale yellow to deep sherry-red. Note that some crystals are practically devoid of inclusions.

Imperial topaz

Brazilian topazes were first discovered in the early part of the 18th century, in the region of Ouro Preto, the former capital of Minas Gerais state. Now that the Soviet Union's deposits have been exhausted, this area has become the world's sole producer of imperial topaz. Large occurrences are in Dom Bosco and Rodrigo Silva. The Vermelhão mine, in the vicinity of the city of Ouro Preto is still the most important occurrence. Recently, in this same region, the Capão Mine in Rodrigo Silva has been activated mechanically. The extraction of imperial topaz there is processed by hydraulic dismounting.

The gemstone's various colours include yellow, orange, champagne and the much-prized sherry-red, which has a faint pinkish hue. The pink type, containing chrome traces, is extremely difficult to find on the market, and is generally reserved for collectors.

Group of imperial topaz crystals surrounding a 27 – carat cut specimen of an intense sherry-red colour (Ouro Preto region, state of Minas Gerais).

Pale yellow topazes, in crystals weighing several kilogrammes, are frequently found in the pegmatites north of Teófilo Otoni. When cut, they give splendid, sparkling gemstones, reminiscent of yellow sapphire.

Deposits of colourless topaz are spread over the pegmatite fields or their alluvium.

Group of imperial topazes, in their various hues (Ouro Preto region, state of Minas Gerais).

Imperial topaz gem crystal (Vermelhão mine, state of Minas Gerais).

Blue topaz

Blue topaz, which resembles aquamarine, although it has a steel-like and more brilliant luster, may be distinguished from the latter also by its higher specific gravity. Always found in pegmatites or their secondary deposits, blue topaz comes mainly from Minas Gerais, in the Jequitinhonha valley (Araçuaí, Barra de Salinas) and in the regions of Teófilo Otoni and Serro. Other deposits are located in Bahia and Espirito Santo states.

Blue topaz with lepidolite – property of the Smithsonian Institution.

A few years ago a pegmatite field located near Virgem da Lapa, in Minas Gerais, became famous for its large blue topazes, often of gem quality. Major deposits here are at Xanda, Limoeiro and Toca da Onça.

These are zoned pegmatites, only slightly inclined and rich in geodes coated with cleavelandite, lepidolite and quartz, set with lovely topazes. Associated are remarkable crystals of apatite and hydroxylherderite, and some beryl, microlite, cassiterite, columbo-tantalite and garnet.

Blue topaz (Virgem da Lapa, Minas Gerais).

Chrysoberyl

One of the most interesting, yet least known, of the important gemstones, chrysoberyl deserves a very special mention for its rarity and astounding beauty. The few deposits outside Brazil are almost worked out, underlining its significance.

Cyclical twin of a complete chrysoberyl (rosette) resembling a dented wheel. (right)

Two chrysoberyls. The stone on the left is a 15 carat alexandrite cat's eye. The other is a beautiful cat's eye chrysoberyl weighing 12 carats, displaying an intense chatoyancy.

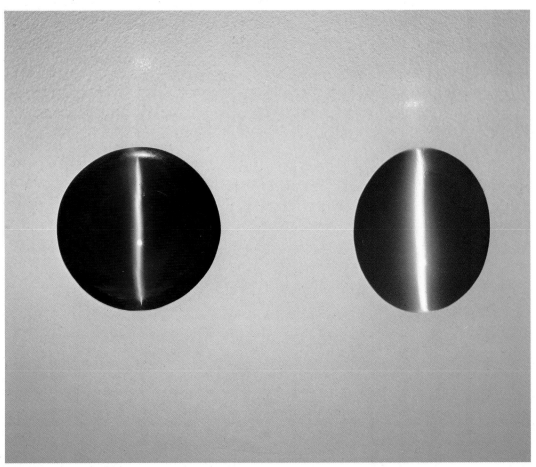

The rare presence of chrome traces in chrysoberyl turns it into alexandrite − a gemstone which can be considered one of the most unique and valuable of all. The stone was named after Czar Alexander II of Russia, an illustrious collector. This chrysoberyl changes colour, passing from soft green in sunlight to deep red in candle or artificial light. The layman can feel difficulty in grasping how a coloured stone, which can easily be mistaken for a green tourmaline by day or a rubellite at night, can fetch astronomical prices. Yet connoisseurs know that the demand for such an exotic stone is ever increasing.

Another of the chrysoberyl's curious aspects is that, contrary to what happens with the majority of other stones, specimens with certain inclusions can reach a higher value than other so-called "pure" gemstones. This phenomenon is due to the presence of fine, fiber-like inclusions, distributed evenly in a certain part of the crystal. Cut into a cabochon, with the girdle parallel to the inclusions plane, such a gemstone presents an extremely striking chatoyant effect, called "cat's eye".

The various chrysoberyl occurrences found to date in Brazil are located in Padre Paraíso (Minas Gerais state), Colatina and Santa Teresa (Espírito Santo state). Some alexandrites, very dark and of little transparency, are found in the Carnaíba emerald mine, in Bahia state.

Flat crystals, in cyclical twins, are sought after avidly by collectors. The transparent ones, however, are systematically cut.

Magnificent translucent alexandrite crystal showing the change of colour phenomena under incandescent and daylight respectively. − Photograph reproduced from "Gemmologia" by Professor Speranza Cavenago-Bignami Moneta.

Under incandescent light.

Under daylight.

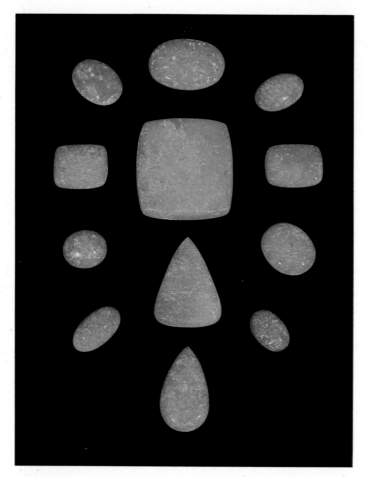

Opal

A mythical aura of mystery and fascination surrounds the precious opal. The play of colour, which emerges from the heart of a fine opal gives it an appearance that has intrigued and mystified man since ancient times. It is the Aurora Borealis, the "southern lights" on a glacial landscape, captured in a soft, fragile stone.

Opal is a hydrated silica with a vitreous appearance, showing traces of magnesium, iron and calcium. It presents an ultra-spherulitic structure, detectable under the electron microscope. The silica spherules, bound in a similar siliceous cement, are grouped within zones of identical diametre, which confers a mosaic aspect. The diffraction of light and variations in refractive index give the opal its famous varied reflections. Even under overcast skies a gem opal displays a dazzling, twinkling palette of radiant colours.

Fragment of a rough slab of Piauí opal from the Boi Morto mine, state of Piauí.

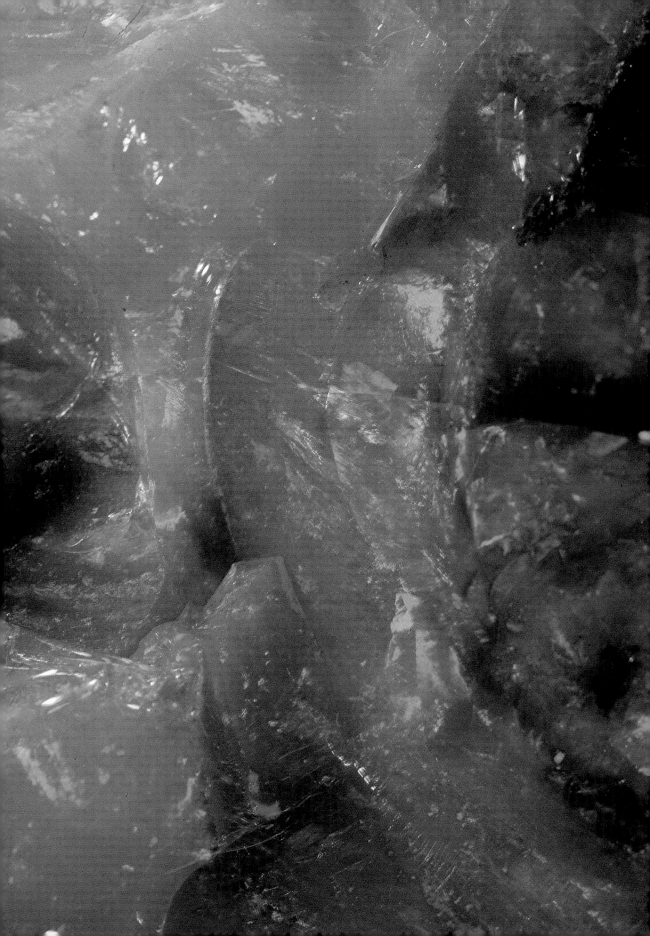

The richest occurrence to date was discovered in Boi Morto, within the municipality of Pedro II, in the state of Piauí. There, basalt sills of the Upper Jurassic period intersect slightly inclined sandstone from the Devonian period. Posterior hydrothermal flows of silica loaded water deposited opal in the rock's cracks and crevices. The gemstone also appears in some more argilaceous sandstone beds which act as a trap. More resistant to erosion than the sandstone where it becomes incrusted, the opal frequently remains in superficial eluvial or colluvial deposits, where it is mined.

Apart from Boi Morto, in this state there are a number of other localities producing opal, of which the most important is Roça, where the first specimens were found in secondary deposits, along a temporarily dried out riverbed. The largest specimen ever found in the region weighed almost one kilogramme, consisting of fine gem quality opal. The mother rock between two layers of sandstone is also being mined nowadays. Opal bearing layers in this area sometimes reach up to 20 centimetres.

Other occurrences in the Pedro II district are Cantinho, Bom Lugar, Limão, Centro, Mamoeiro, Morro do Meio and Barra.

The bulk production of Piaui's precious opal has a white translucent to semi-transparent body colour. Some stones originating from Roça have an orange body base. In 1974 a Boi Morto vein yielded a small quantity of black opal.

The finer specimens of Piaui's opals can easily be mistaken for the best-quality specimens from Australia. The relatively low water content of Brazilian opals (5.7%) – against the usual 10% in opals from other provenances – explains why even prolonged exposure to heat, such as, on lighted window displays, does not crack them.

The absence of inclusions and fractures in conjunction with the evenness of the play of colour's layers allow the fashioning of large cabochons, sometimes attaining a 60 millimetres diametre.

Some scattered fire-opal fragments were found in Lageado, in Rio Grande do Sul state, associated with amethyst. Their colour varies from lemon-yellow orange, to red-brown. Unfortunately, these opals show no multiple play of colour. New occurrences of fire-opals with play of colour can be expected in this region, which is still only partly explored geologically.

Some green opals have been found in the Boa Nova municipality, in Bahia state. Milky and hyaline opals are common in the Northeast scheelite occurrences (Currais Novos, state of Rio Grande do Norte) and in lead deposits (Boquira, Bahia state).

Mounted set of opals of extraordinary beauty, from Pedro II, state of Piauí.

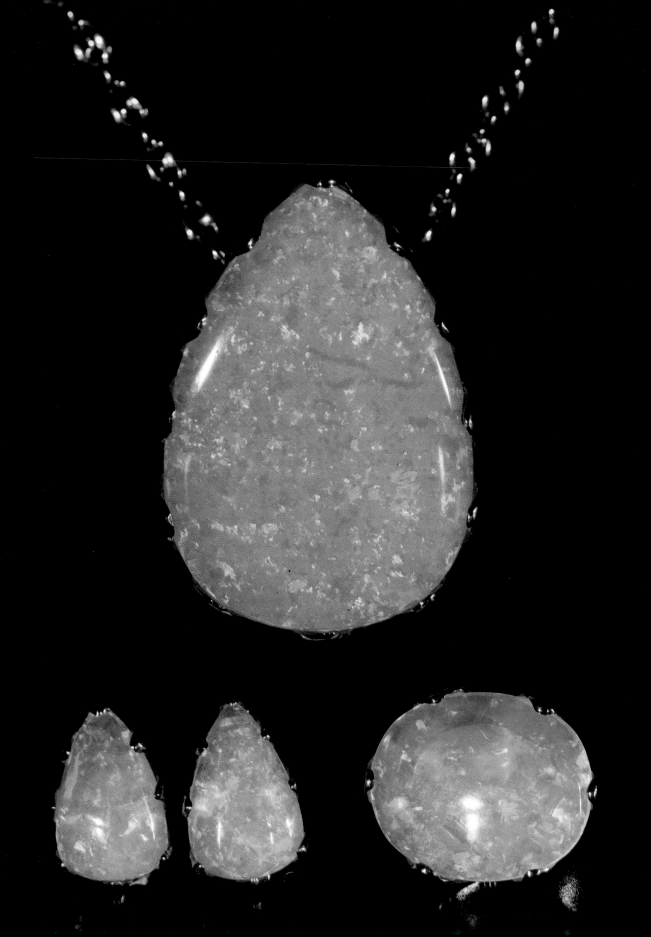

Kunzites of various shapes and hues, from Córrego do Urucum, state of Minas Gerais.

Kunzite group, mounted in gold and diamonds. The stones come from the Urucum mine (Galiléia municipality, state of Minas Gerais) and were found in 1964.

Spodumene

Although spodumene is an industrial lithium mineral widespread around the world, only two of its varieties are of gem quality: the pink-violet, kunzite, and the green, hiddenite. Only four gem spodumene deposits exist on the planet.

Gem crystals sometimes attain ten centimetres. They are flattened vertically, with a roof-shaped extremity, and show easily-developed cleavage. However, once the ideal faceting angle is found, there is practically no danger of posterior cleaving.

In Brazil, two pegmatites were discovered in 1962 which produced very large quantities of splendid kunzite and a few hiddenite crystals. One of the occurrences is situated at Córrego do Urucum, near Galiléia, in the Doce river region, in Minas Gerais state. A pegmatite situated between granite and mica-schist concealed an enormous geode coated with kunzite and morganite crystals averaging 50 centimetres. The gemstones were accompanied by quartz with tourmaline needles, coloured tourmalines, garnets, lepidolite and columbite. The second deposit, known as Fazenda Anglo, near Itambacuri, also in Minas Gerais state, has equally produced excellent kunzites. Both deposits are now in a state of collapse, but Urucum is presently being cleared again.

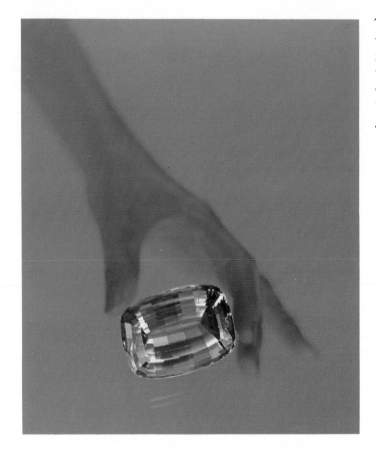

The name "kunzite" was given to honour the great gemologist George F. Kunz, who at the beginning of the century travelled around the world seeking gemstones for great collectors, such as American banker J.P. Morgan. At the time, Brazil was still unknown as a gem producer, and the most coveted kunzites came from California and the Carolinas. After kunzites were discovered in Brazil, collectors and museums were anxious to acquire Brazilian specimens, outstanding in their beauty and size.

Gem kunzite, from the Urucum mine, state of Minas Gerais. Weight: 530 carats.

Spodumene of the hiddenite variety. (left)

Kunzite from the Urucum mine, state of Minas Gerais. (right)

Brazilianite

In the field of gemology, the dream of any researcher is to discover a new mineral. In 1943, a sodium aluminium phosphate turned up in a pegmatite known as Córrego Frio, near Linópolis, east of Governador Valadares, state of Minas Gerais; at first, garimpeiros thought they had found chrysoberyl crystals.

When this mineral proved to be a new species – which caused a great sensation at the time – it was called brazilianite, in homage to Brazil.
Throughout the years, other small pegmatites, in neighbouring deposits, also yielded the mineral, all upstream of the Laranjeiras river, state of Minas Gerais.

Brazilianite ranges from colourless to golden yellow, with brown varieties of a green or yellow hue. With a hardness of 5.5 and rarely found without inclusions, it is only cut on a small scale, and greatly appreciated by collectors in its natural form.

Two brazilianite crystals, with cleavelandite, from Córrego Frio, state of Minas Gerais.

Brazilianite crystal agglomerate, which illustrated the cover of the February 1974 Lapidary Journal magazine. From the Telírio mine, state of Minas Gerais. Weight: eight kilogrammes.

Quartz

Amethyst

Amethyst is the most prized member of the quartz family. Despite abundant supply it has never lost its value or gone out of fashion.

Its name comes from the Greek "amethustos", meaning "not drunken" - a reference to its supposed quality of preventing the owner from getting drunk. Historical references include a mention in the Bible of amethyst as one of the ten stones on which the names of the tribes of Israel were engraved.

Formerly the exclusive preserve of the nobility and church, it has fortunately become more widely available. No longer is it necessary to be Catherine the Great of Russia to possess this gem.

In its natural state fine zones of intense violet colour alternate with colourless bands, distributed in parallel. This is a way to discern the genuine article from the imitation, common because of its popularity. Like most gemstones, the amethyst's value increases with the density of its colour, as long as transparency remains unaffected.

The discovery, last century, of fabulous amethyst deposits in Brazil has dwarfed any existing previously. Main deposits are located in the states of Rio Grande do Sul, Mato Grosso do Sul, Minas Gerais, Espírito Santo, Goiás, Bahia and Ceará. However, the amethyst is not normally found in pegmatites and thus Minas Gerais, Brazil's foremost gem-producing state, is bereft of this particular species.

Amethysts are found in isolated crystals, which can reach more than a dozen centimetres in length, or else in groups of extremely variable size, where only the pyramid tips are salient. In most cases only the top extremity is coloured, the base being hyaline or milky. The crystals frequently form polysynthetic twins: many of which, lacking prismatic form, only display the terminal rhombohedral pyramids.

Radiated amethyst slab with agate centre (Iraí, state of Rio Grande do Sul).

Bowl, cut from a gigantic crystal originally weighing more than 28 kilogrammes (Jacobina mine, state of Bahia). (right)

Amethyst-citrine displays the two noblest representatives of the quartz species in one single stone (found in 1981, state of Mato Grosso do Sul).

The colour is generally due to an iron ion in an abnormal electrical state. The coloured layers are mostly distributed in an irregular manner, as a result of growth peculiarities or of the formation of twins. The growth planes parallel to the rhombohedron faces have the deepest colour. The colour thus concentrates either in certain sectors of the crystal or in a series of parallel dihedra.

Brazil's amethyst deposits vary considerably. The most important specimens come from the Paraná basin, but the main production centre is situated in Rio Grande do Sul state, on a plateau where fissural eruptions during the Mesozoic age affected more than half a million square kilometres. The druses are often irregular or elongated, and can reach more than a cubic metre in volume. They are lined with amethyst, sometimes accompanied by calcite or zeolite. Druses are in general covered with a layer of delessite, making their origin easier to determine. The main mining centres are found in the outskirts of São Gabriel, near Iraí. Also noteworthy are Lageado, Encantado, Espumoso, Soledade and São Borja.

82

Alluvial and eluvial deposits are generally small and have a limited production. An outstanding exception is the Brejinho das Ametistas deposit, in the Caetité region, state of Bahia, situated in a vast colluvial bed on the lower eastern slopes of the Espinhaço range, locally known as the "amethysts range".

Veins and stockwerks intersecting the metamorphic rocks are equally abundant and produce gem amethysts. They are mainly found in Minas Gerais and Bahia states.

Giant crystal, clearly showing natural amethyst colour zoning. Weighs over four kilogrammes.

The Lavra do Coxo deposit, otherwise known as Jacobina, is perhaps the most beautiful and grandiose in Brazil. It is located west-northwest of Salvador in the centre of Bahia state. The landscape is formed by towering quartzite ranges, separated by deep valleys, part of the "Supergrupo Minas" geological complex. Discovered more than fifty years ago, the deposit coincides with a vertical sheared zone, parallel to the regional vector, where gigantic quartzite blocks tumbled over each other. The cavities of this mind-bogglling chaos are lined with amethyst, in layers frequently covering more than several dozen square metres. Crystals of diametres often exceeding ten centimetres, display a deep violet colour, verging on black, in their upper extremity. The base ranges from hyaline to translucent, with hematite and pyrite rims. Most crystals are of superlative quality, and easy to separate from the gangue.

Finally, part-amethyst, part-citrine crystals have recently been discovered in Mato Grosso do Sul state; the amethyst proportion predominates.

Mammilary druse covered with amethyst crystals, more appreciated by collectors than geodes with inner lining.

100-carat amethyst necklace mounted in gold and diamonds.

Arborescent citrine cluster on a quartzite base.

Citrine

Citrine is a quartz variety, like amethyst and rock crystal, with which it is normally associated. The mineral's name comes from its luminous lemon colour, ranging from light yellow to gold-brown. The colouring is explained by the presence of iron in the state of trivalent ions and of ultra-microscopic precipitations of ferrous oxyde. The characteristic colour banding can be concealed in the cut gem, most of the times, specially when large crystals are available to the artisan.

Brazil is the primary source of this gemstone.

During the 1940s large citrine deposits were found in Minas Gerais state. The two main occurrences are at Campo Belo and Sete Lagoas, where magnificent, inclusion-free specimens of up to a kilogramme have been found.

Beautiful prism ending in a hexagonal pyramid, ox-blood red colour, from Campo Belo, state of Minas Gerais and a cut stone from the same region.

Set of citrines (Iraí, state of Rio Grande do Sul).

Other deposits where citrine is found, always along with rock crystal and smoky quartz, are:
    Minas Gerais: Bom Despacho, Diamantina, Conselheiro Mota, Salinas;
    Goiás: Catalão, Cristalina, Serra dos Cristais and Santa Luzia;
    Espírito Santo: the Baixo Guandu region;
    Bahia: Caetité and Xique-Xique.
A temporary paralyzation of many of the mentioned deposits has caused a shortage. Citrine is not very common in its natural state. Most cut citrine comes from the thermic treatment of amethysts. This treatment, which can sometimes be observed in nature itself, consists of heating the stone to 550°C. The process is irreversible and only a small percentage of crystals resist the colour change.

For the layman, this stone can easily pass for imperial topaz, because of the strong similarity of colour. The distinguishing features are several, such as, crystallographic system, specific gravity and optical density.

The carat value of a fine colour citrine does not surpass 10% of that of a similar grade imperial topaz.

Heat-treated citrines (Iraí, state of Rio Grande do Sul).

Transparent smoky quartz of the "cathedral" type.

Citrine cluster in the form of a pineapple (Iraí, state of Rio Grande do Sul).

Longitudinal, arborescent group of small rock crystals (outskirts of Diamantina, state of Minas Gerais).

Other quartzes

Quartz is undoubtedly one of the most common minerals found in nature, and probably the most extensively used. The mineral's resistance to heat and chemical inertia has given it an essential role in modern industry, particularly in electronics and optics.

Quartz was instrumental in boosting Brazil's mineral industry. Strategic demand made it the world's top producer during the Second World War. Simultaneously, mining operations brought to light, in great quantity, associated gemstones which would not have been found otherwise.

Quartz has often been useful in that the steady demand for this product has been able to support a mine primarily concerned with a more valuable gem at an early stage of development, or else where gemstone production had been temporarily interrupted.

Beautiful crystals are always in great demand by collectors. Furthermore, most specimens of other minerals increase in value when grown on a quartz base.

There are innumerable deposits around the world, in diverse forms: veins, lenses, pegmatites, segregations and alluvium. Quartz deposits tend to be located in Upper Pre-Cambrian and older "Supergrupo Minas" fields. Gigantic quartz, sometimes perfect, is usually found in pegmatites; true marvels of nature in dimension and transparency. The world record quartz crystal specimen, weighing 5.500 kilogrammes comes from Minas Gerais state, which has produced the largest quantity of quartz crystals of all times.

Quartz, an oxide of silicon, generally crystallizes in hexagonal prisms, ended by hexagonal or trigonal pyramids. An infinity of other forms, exist. Besides incrustations and inclusions common to other gemstones, a variety of metallic inclusions, such as pyrite and hemative, exist. Many of the so-called "impurities" found in quartz are really a mosaic of exquisite inclusions and sometimes even increase the specimen's value.

Art objects in rock crystal, from the Harold and Erica Van Pelt collection.

A variety of reddish-chestnut quartz, called hematoid, has been known for a long time in Europe, originating from Santiago de Compostella, Spain, It was much appreciated by the pilgrims, who took it home as travel memento. A few years ago, marvelous groups of hematoid quartz crystals were discovered in the Jacobina amethyst mine, state, of Bahia.

Quartz cannot always be used for gemological purposes, as the crystals are usually translucent and with no potential beauty. Besides the noblest varieties, amethyst and citrine, transparent varieties (rock crystal, smoky, iris, rutilated quartz) and semi-transparent to opaque varieties (rose quartz, aventurine and blue quartz) are used in jewelry, art objects and ornaments.

Open rose of crystallized quartz (Jequitinhonha river island mine, state of Minas Gerais). (right)

Hematoid quartz agglomerate (Jacobina Mine, state of Bahia)

Rose quartz owes its attractive colour to the presence of titanium in the state of trivalent ions. This metal can also precipitate in the form of microscopic rutile needles, arranged according to the crystal's binary rhombohedric axes. An asterism effect is obtained by correct cutting.

Rose quartz occurs in large xenomorphic masses in differentiated pegmatites, where they can form accumulations of several dozen tons, among gigantic feldspar crystals. Important deposits are in Piabanha, near Joaíma (Minas Gerais), Alto Feio, near Pedra Lavrada (Paraíba) and the Ribeirão do Largo and Macarani pegmatites (Bahia).

Unlike large masses of xenomorphic quartz, naturally facetted rose quartz crystals are very rare. Almost certainly Brazil is the world's sole producer. Two localities must be mentioned, both in Minas Gerais: the Sapucaia deposit (near Divino das Laranjeiras) and the Jequitinhonha river island (near Itinga). The latter is about 200 kilometres north of the first occurrence. Relatively recent, these discoveries have enriched public and private collections. Specimens from both places illustrate this book.

Green quartz forms thick layers in the quartzites of the Diamantina plateau (Minas Gerais), in Jacobina and on the Planalto Baiano, near Belo Campo (Bahia). To date, only the intense green type, aventurine, has been used by the jewellery industry.

The only region where blue quartz masses are found is Boquira, in the arid interior of Bahia. Only the more coloured fragments are used for various types of ornaments. This mineral is in fact quartzite coloured by dumortierite.

A rare specimen of naturally faceted rose quartz with green tourmaline incrustations (Sapucaia, state of Minas Gerais).

One of the most prized varieties is rutilated quartz, sometimes also known as "Venus hair" or "flèches d'amour". Golden fibres form long yellow or red needles. This quartz, of which Brazil is the main producer, is much used for ornamental objects and is particularly desired by collectors. The most famous deposit lies in a small area near Ibitiara, in Bahia. In veins of milky quartz, geodes contain groups of magnificent rutilated quartz crystal, frequently in the company of hexagonal slabs of specularite. In this region, elluvial layers also supply excellent specimens. The crystals, often perfect, can exceed several kilogrammes. In some localities near Diamantina, Minas Gerais, the rutile has a blood-red colour, and is richer in iron than the Ibitiara variety.

Rock crystal vase in rutilated quartz, sculpted by Harold Van Pelt.

"Rutilated quartz − reproduced from 'Internal World of Gem- stones', by Professor E. Gubelin."

Chalcedony (agate)

The small but famous Idar-Oberstein agate deposits, mined since the 15th century, gave birth to local stone-cutting workshops, which made this town one of the most prosperous in Germany. These deposits were worked out last century. Lured by immense agate deposits covering over a million square kilometres, German immigrants flocked to southern Brazil.

Agate, a variety of chalcedony, can be found in numerous countries, but no deposits can compare with those in Brazil for quality, size of nodules and the dimension of its producing areas. Agate from Rio Grande do Sul state is preferred over any other for the manufacture of jewels and ornaments, especially in Western countries.

Chalcedony comes mostly in the form of mammillary concretions with a radiated fibre structure. These anhydrous silica fibres, with a composition close to quartz, are surrounded by an amorphous, silicic cement. The physical properties of chalcedony are comparable to those of quartz, though slightly inferior. Chalcedony was formed by the alteration, mainly through leaching of rock containing silica.

Agates are composed of successive layers in varying thickness and different colours of chalcedony, concentrically arranged. There is a continuous transition from chalcedony to agate. The latter appears in nodules of various sizes and contains a series of banded layers.

According to their appearance and characteristics, agates are termed "landscape", "layer", "moss" or "fortification". Ashtrays, plates, bowls and other ornamental objects are made by cutting and polishing the better quality agates.

Due to their porous nature, many agates can be dyed in a wide spectrum of colours. Once dyed they are known in Brazil as "umbu".

Agate plate showing angular zoning, in a picturesque arrangement, reminiscent of a tunnel. The magnificent colour spectrum is natural.

Extremely varied, natural colour agates from Rio Grande do Sul state, come in rounded nodules, which can weigh up to several dozen kilogrammes. Just like amethysts, they are also found in lava fields in various stages of decomposition, but never in association with each other. Mining is partly mechanized, through the use of explosives or rippers to remove the overburden. Highly resistant to erosion, agates are either concentrated on the surface of the ground, where they were mined in the past, or else in rivers.

Mining centres are many. Among them are Alegrete, Camagá, Dom Pedrito, Livramento, Passo Fundo, Guaraí, Rio Pardo, Rio Taquari, Santa Maria, São Borja, São Gabriel, Três Cruzes and Uruguaiana.

At present, the main production centre is located in the outskirts of Salto Grande, on the banks of the Jacuí river. Agates in the area are particularly susceptible to dyes of various colours. The material extracted has a low market value, which only increases after cutting and polishing. Some agates are brownish, like those in the region of Três Pinheiros, Fontoura-Xavier and Soledade, where mining is also very intensive.

Various other Brazilian states produce agates. The Municipality of Contendas do Sincorá, boasts a superb finely grained red jasper, forming a layer several metres thick in the quartzite of the Diamantina plateau.

Bahia: Brumado, Conquista, Rio das Contas;

Ceará: Barbalha, Canindé, Tauá;

Espírito Santo: Castelo (Fazenda Santa Helena);

Mato Grosso: the Cuiabá river upstream from the capital and the Pardo and Paraná rivers;

Minas Gerais: Araçuaí, Diamantina, Patrocínio, Salinas, Teófilo Otoni, Uberaba;

Paraíba: Picuí.

Translucent agate plate, with chromatic nodules.

Finally, on the surface of agate deposits, it is common to find delicate formations with varied shapes, often multilobular, composed of single or clustered chalcedony discs, undulated and peppered with small quartz crystals. Known as "quartz rose", they are used for decoration or jewellery.

A century after the discovery of Brazilian agate, this immense mineral reserve has barely been tapped, as priority has been given to gemstones of higher value. In Brazil, the transformation of agates into jewelry on a wider scale will probably only take place in future generations.

Shell-like chalcedony formation.

Group of art objects in Brazilian agate, belonging to Harold Van Pelt.

Garnet

The garnet is composed of a number of closely related mineral species, varying slightly in chemical composition being referred to as the garnet group.

With the development of gemstone mining in Brazil, deposits of several garnet varieties have been discovered in ever-increasing numbers, particularly pyrope, almandine, spessartite, grossular and andradite. Brazilian deposits are of three types: in pegmatites, in mica schists and in alluvium. In pegmatites, the garnet comes in isolated crystals or in massive aggregates, which can exceed ten kilogrammes. They are always found in the company of other industrial minerals, near the quartz core. In mica schists, the garnet appears in crystals, sometimes very large (five kilogrammes, near Veneza, state of Pernambuco) generally in a rhombo-dedecahedron shape. The schists are intersected by various eruptive dykes and quartz veins, which yield beautiful garnets (Parelhas, state of Rio Grande do Norte). In alluvial deposits garnets are often found with other precious stones, such as aquamarines and tourmalines.

The main deposits and occurrences are, in each state:
– Bahia: Andaraí, Caetité, Feira de Santana, Macugê, Mundo Novo, Santo Antônio and Utinga;
– Ceará: Icó, Orós, Quizeramobim, Quixadá, and specially the famous pegmatite deposit of Poço dos Cavalos, presently flooded, from where magnificent garnets originate, of a fringe composition between almandine and spessartite.
– Espírito Santo: Colatina, Itapemirim, Rio Piúma and Santa Tereza.
– Minas Gerais: the most beautiful garnets come from Resplendor and Barra do Coité. Other deposits are Abaeté, Aiuroca, Antônio Pereira, Araçuaí, Conselheiro Pena, Gravatá, Itinga, Minas Novas, Santa Maria, São José de Brejaúbas, all yielding almandine and spessartite. Finally the Ribeirão Lava-Pés pegmatite, near Poaiá, produces splendid garnets, also of a fringe composition between almandine and spessartite. Barbacena, Entre-Rios and Queluz, as well as Morro da Mina, near Lafaiete, yield an abundance of spessartites.

The pyrope essentially comes from norther Minas Gerais. Other locations are:
– Paraíba: Santa Luzia, Pedra Branca, Pedra Lavada and Piauí;
– Pernambuco: the Veneza and Boa Vista regions;
– Rio Grande do Norte: the Currais Novos region (grossular), Martins, Parelhas, São João do Sabugi, Seridó and Serra Negra.

Presently only the Poaiá mine is in activity, due to the existence of particularly rare massive blocks of garnets which produce the so-called "eyes" suitable for fashioning. Sizes are under three carats. Some unsually larges "eyes" have been uncovered which yield up to 15 carats of totally transparent garnets, with colours ranging from yellow to cognac.

Due to its superbly high refractive index, the garnet can be considered a much-desired precious stone, in its rarer specimens.

Hessonite from the Bodó scheelite mine, state of Rio Grande do Norte property of Prof. J. Cassedanne.

Various fashioned garnets.

Collection stones

Ambligonite

As far as known, no gem quality amblygonite was found in Brazil or any part of the world before 1975. That year, partially transparent crystals were unearthed near Itinga, in Lavra Velha, state of Minas Gerais. They were fit to be cut into incredibly large gemstones of up to one hundred carats, and were practically devoid of inclusions. Colour, especially in the larger specimens, is a superb, intense chartreuse. In 1977 another gem quality amblygonite deposit was found in Lavra do Telírio, near Linópolis, state of Minas Gerais.

Andalusite

Andalusite, with a hardness of 7.5, and a very strong pleochroism, in green and pink hues, allows the cutter to enhance its originality to such a point that it can almost be compared to the alexandrite, in its change of colour phenomena. Andalusites over five carats fetch handsome prices. Brazil produces some in the Santa Teresa and Itaguaçu regions of the state of Espírito Santo and near Itinga, in the Jequitinhonha region, in the state of Minas Gerais.

Diopside

Diopside is a calcium-magnesium silicate. The density of colour hues varies according to the amount of ferrous iron in replacement to the magnesium.
Cabochons are obtained from fibrous chatoyant and four-rayed star varieties.

The transparent gem variety is more often acquired by collectors since the perfect prismatic cleavage and the low hardness compromise its wearability.
The mineral is frequently found in contact metamorphic rocks and comes in crystals exceeding ten centimetres (tactites of the Northeast, for instance).

On the other hand, there are few deposits yielding cuttable stones, all in the state of Minas Gerais. Some worth mentioning are Araçuaí, Bom Sucesso, Conceição do Serro and Salinas. Near Malacacheta, in the Aguas Quentes district, thick chromodiopside layers associated with quartz produce beautifully coloured gem crystals.

Epidote

In 1976, a substantially rich epidote deposit was discovered in the Santa Maria municipality, state of Pernambuco, yielding crystals of up to ten grammes. At first, the garimpeiros thought that they had stumbled upon a new emerald occurrence, which caused a rush to the locality. On finding out, however, that they were dealing with epidote, they abandoned the deposit, to this day.

First row: Fluorite, Titanite, Calcite
Second row: Apatite, Andalusite, Kyanite
Third row: Zircon, Brown tourmaline, Phenakite
Fourth row: Iolite, Euclase, Sphalerite
Fifth row: Lazulite, Olivine, Alexandrite

Euclase

The euclase, particularly the blue variety, is found along with imperial topaz in the Ouro Preto region. Collectors have always been extremely fond of this stone. Double-terminated uncut crystals, when free of inclusions, fetch sometimes higher prices than cut stones. Elsewhere, colourless crystals several centimetres long can be found in the Santana do Encoberto area, near São Sebastião do Maranhão, state of Minas Gerais. Another euclase deposit, associated with industrial beryl, lies near Equador, in Alto do Giz, state of Rio Grande do Norte.

Fluorite

Fluorite is a fluoride of calcium crystallized in the cubic system. A wide variety of colours with usually light tones are typical of this mineral. The easily developped octahedral cleavage and the low hardness make it unsuitable for jewelry. Massive crystals are carved into ornamental objects and transparent coloured crystals are faceted for collectors. There are many fluorite deposits in Brazil. However, few produce stones suitable for ornamental objects.

In the Ramalho range, state of Bahia, blue and violet slabs are embedded in the Bambuí calcareous formations. The Salgadinho pegmatite near Santa Luzia, state of Paraíba, has beautiful transparent green octahedral crystals. In the Criscíúma, Urussanga, Tubarão areas of the state of Santa Catarina, several deposits produce fluorite in striped blocks which are cuttable. Yellow and beige colours predominate, with blue or green strips. Finally, near Rio Bonito, state of Rio de Janeiro, a lovely golden fluorite is mined in large blocks.

Hematite

The most important iron ore, hematite is used in jewelry, such as, cameos, intaglios, beads and cabochons. Its high metallic sheen contrasting with its opacity has attracted mankind since ancient times. The name derives from the Greek – blood – due to its blood-coloured dust. A faceted hematite has an appearance similar to that of the rare black diamond.

Iron ore deposits are countless in Brazil. The hematite used in jewelry comes from the state of Minas Gerais (the iron-producing polygon: Dom Bosco, Itabira, Miguel Burnier, Antonio Pereira, Cachoeira do Campo) and Bahia (Brumado and Rio das Contas).

First row: Scapolite, Brazilianite, Indicolite
Second row: Petalite, Epidote, Diopside
Third row: Apophyllite Heliodor, Tantalite
Fourth row: Morganite, Schorl, Achroite

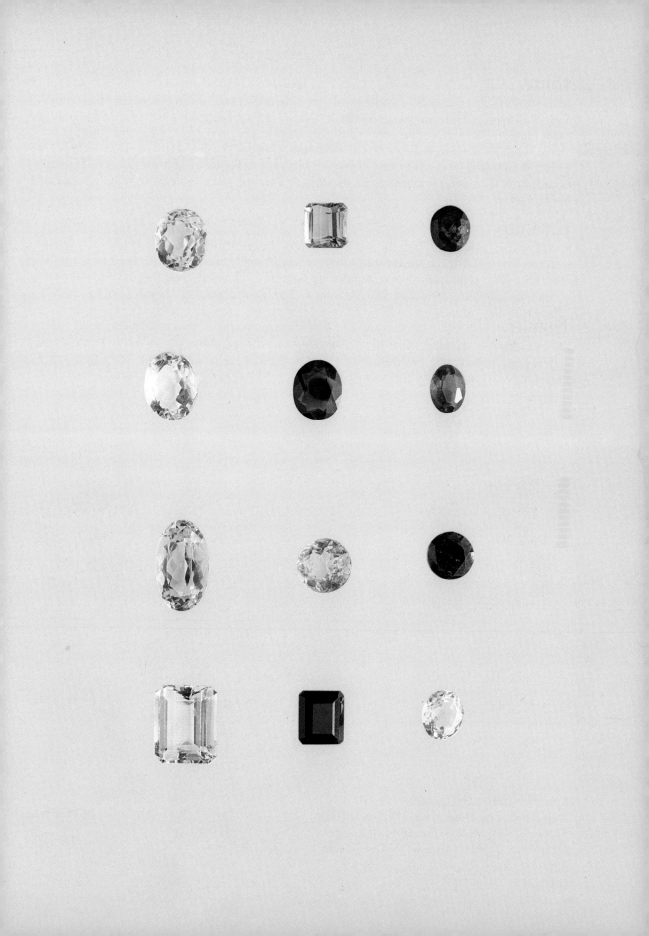

Iolite

Also known as cordierite or dichroite, it is best known among jewelers and gemologists as iolite. With an attractive blue colour, strong pleochroism and fair durability, the iolite could easily become a popular gemstone if there would be sufficient production.

This metamorphic mineral is very common but gem deposits are extremely rare. To date, occurrences have been found near Picuí, state of Paraíba, and close to Virgolândia, state of Minas Gerais.

Kyanite

Kyanite, like andalusite, has the same chemical composition but with a different crystal structure. It also displays an intense pleochroism. A cabochon cut will bring out an admirable chatoyant effect. Many occurrences are located in Brumado and Rio das Contas, state of Bahia, Capelinha, state of Minas Gerais, and in the state of Mato Grosso do Sul.

Lazulite

Despite being a relatively common mineral found in quartzites and in some pegmatites, gem lazulite is quite rare in desirable size and without fractures. The main known region is the Espinhaço range in the states of Minas Gerais and Bahia, especially around Diamantina.

First row: Hematite, Dendritic Quartz
Second row: Blue Quartz, Fire Opal, Lepidolite
Third row: Aventurine, Turquoise, Moonstone
Fourth row: Saphire, Amazonite, Ambligonite
Fifth row: Ruby, Hessonite, Quartz "Fumé"

Peridot

The peridot was probably the most wellknown gemstone in antiquity. Its most valuable variety has a medium-dark yellowish green colour a displaying velvety texture, due to its strong birefringence.

In Brazil, the best samples come from Bom Sucesso, Teófilo Otoni and Conceição do Serro, state of Minas Gerais.

Petalite

Gem quality petalite was only found recently in Brazil, while mining the mineral for industrial purposes. The occurrence is located around Taquaral on the Piauí river, west of the Rio-Salvador highway, in the Jequitinhonha valley, state of Minas Gerais.
The rare transparent colourless crystals, devoid of inclusions are very much appreciated by collectors.

Scapolite

Scapolites, otherwise known as wernerites, are sodium-calcium feldspathic minerals. There are large anions in their structural pattern: chlorine, sulphate, etc... A continuous series stretches between the two extremes: marialite and meionite. Intermediates are called dipire (sodic) and scapolite (calcic). Its physical constants are close to feldspars: three-dimensional, easily-developed cleavage, hardness 6, low specific gravity and refractive index.

Transparent, dichroic, yellow scapolite can resemble the clear citrine. Ultraviolet rays bring out a lilac luminescence. Scapolite is an abundant mineral in contact deposits, especially in the Northeast's scheelite layers, where it sometimes comes in prisms over ten centimetres long. However, it is rarely transparent or cuttable. The Antonio Coelho mine, near Itaguaçu, state of Espírito Santo, has produced transparent yellow stones.

Apophyllite and stilbite, from the Antas tunnel, state of Rio Grande do Sul.

Sphalerite

The sphalerite's attraction is its extremely high refractive index. The frequently used brilliant cut enhances this stone's extraordinary brilliance. Its low hardness of 4 and the perfect dodecahedral cleavage do not recommend it for the use in jewelry.

Occurrences known to date are Fazenda das Macaúbas, near Tiros, and Jazida da Mina Grande, near Itacarambi, state of Minas Gerais.

Sphene (Titanite)

An extraordinary fire makes this stone particularly fascinating, when transparent, and can easily be mistaken for an extremely rare "chartreuse" diamond. However, due to its low hardness, its use in conventional jewelry is not recommended. Nevertheless it is a definite must for collectors. The main source is in Campo do Boa, near the city of Capelinha, state of Minas Gerais.

Turquoise

In a place called Serrote da Lagoa Sêca, near the tiny village of Casa Nova, state of Bahia, a turquoise vein cut the local Pre-cambrian gneiss. This deposit, the first to be discovered in Brazil, was flooded by the waters of the Sobradinho dam. The turquoise was associated with other phosphates, such as variscite.

Zircon

For years zircon has been used by jewelers as the best natural substitute for the diamond, due to its adamantine lustre and fire. Although zircon is very common in pegmatites as well as in alkaline chimneys in Brazil, gem quality deposits are rare. The major is in Rio Verdinho, near Poços de Caldas, state of Minas Gerais. Occasionally, gem zircon can also be found in the states of Espírito Santo and Rio Grande do Norte.

Some opaque crystals from the Rio das Mortes valley, state of Goiás, are mainly sought after by collectors, because of their exceptional dimensions, sometimes attaining several centimetres.

Turquoise on matrix extracted during the Sobradinho dam excavation works, state of Bahia. Weight: 56 kilogrammes.

Apatite

Apatite is a calcium fluoro- and chloro-phosphate, very common in crystalline rock. Its crystal pattern is hexagonal. Gem crystals are always quite small, with relatively low hardness and refractive index. However, its lively, beautiful colours make this gemstone a great favourite among collectors.

Yellow apatites is found in deposits around Gavião-Riachão de Jacuípe, state of Bahia. These deposits are otherwise famous for their splendid crystals, several centimetres long, often terminated, of a dark blue reminiscent of sapphire. Green and bluish-green stones are also mined from a tactite in the Afogados da Ingazeira region, state of Paraíba.

Pink apatite is found in geodes of the Morro Velho gold mine, state of Minas Gerais. The most recent discovery was made in a pegmatite near Governador Valadares, in the same state.

Gem apatite, in quartz and feldspar.

The reddish crystal at the centre of the agglomerate is a gem quality scheelite. Its diameter exceeds one centimetre. Absence of fluorescence seems to indicate a new species.

Calcite – Calcium carbonate is widespread in nature, either in rhombohedric form – cal -
cite – or in orthorhombic form – aragonite – the essential component of pearls.
The constituent element of calcareous rock, its outcrops cover extensive surfaces of Brazil
(São Francisco river basin, Apodi plateau, on the coastline of Sergipe and Alagoas state).
They are often pierced by famous caves (Lapinha, Maquiné, Ubajara, Caverna do Diabo).
When transparent and in large rhombohedra, calcite displays visible strong double refraction:
in other words, a line seem through a crystal's larger facets gives the impression of being two.
This property is much used in optics, and more specifically in gemology.

Lepidolite – A complex lithium, aluminium and potassium silicate, lepidolite
displays a striking pinkish, violet or purple colour. This important lithium mineral is
abundant in certain differentiated pegmatites (with amblygonite, petalite, spodumene),
in crystalline rock of the "greisen" variety and in leucogranites.
Near the Piauí river, in the Araçuaí municipality, the José da Silva deposit produces large
crystals, several dozen centimetres long, and so compact that they can be sculpted into
ornamental objects. Some exceptional crystals from the same deposit show translucency
across the mass when intensely illuminated: the colour thus obtained is a dark, slightly
purplish red, and withstands comparison with antique stained glass.

Amethyst geode, with calcite cen-
tre, from the São Gabriel mine,
state of Rio Grande do Sul.

Gem lepidolite, from the Cruzeiro
mine, state of Minas Gerais.

Corundums

Ruby

A rhombohedral aluminium oxide, the ruby is the most important member of the corundum family. Gem quality is seldomly found, even in traditional places, such as, Burma and Sri Lanka.

Few gem specimens were found to-date in Brazil. These come from Sítio da Jibóia deposit, near Barra Ingedinho, one hundred kilometres from the Vitória da Conquista municipality, state of Bahia. The partially translucent, hexagonal crystals found there are suitable for cabochons, and some have excellent colour. Other places are being surveyed in the states of Minas Gerais (the Guanhães region), Bahia (Jacobina) and Mato Grosso. Opaque pink varieties of corundum are relatively common. Some small gem quality crystals only appear in diamond alluvial deposits (Paraguaçu and Coxim rivers and the Triângulo Mineiro, state of Minas Gerais).

Due to the enormous interest in this gemstone, research efforts are presently being made. The stone's skyrocketing value has made such attempts financially worthwhile, since even small transparent crystals attain attractive prices.

Sapphire

Like the ruby, mainly found in opaque, semi-translucent crystals, solely fit for the cabochon cut, gem-quality transparent sapphire is unknown in Brazil. In 1970 an occurrence near Capim Grosso, state of Bahia, yielded some hundreds of kilogrammes, in size and quality very similar to the ruby found in Sítio da Jibóia.

The navy-blue masses come from the state of Mato Grosso, but their exact origin is unknown. Near Rio de Janeiro, crystals several centimetres long are common, and come from a decomposed leuchtenbergite dyke.

Small sapphire granules turn up in the diamond alluvial deposits of the states of Minas Gerais (Datas, Diamantina, the Sapucaí-Mirim river), Bahia (Salobro river), Mato Grosso (Coxim river) and São Paulo (Itaqui range).

Amazonite crystal, from the Mantena area, state of Minas Gerais.

Sculptures in "gemmy" material

The artistic potential of "gemmy" material can easily be judged from this sculpture. It illustrates the possibilities which giant crystals present in their natural state.

Until recently these were automatically broken up into tiny fragments so as to find that part which showed sufficient transparency for cutting. However, a new awareness of the intrinsic beauty of these objects, as potential works of art in their own right, is beginning to emerge in Brazil. Exciting possibilities for a new industry of considerable significance could be opened up by the widespread use of these techniques and the fact that the crystals are found in almost unlimited quantities in Brazil.

Sculpture in emerald from the Carnaíba mine, state of Bahia, measuring 15x10x8 centimetres.

Group of owls carved from rock crystal, rose quartz, rutilated quartz, amethyst, aquamarine, agate and sodalite.

Ashtray collection, clockwise from left: green tourmaline, rutilated quartz, bicoloured tourmaline, cat's eye rubellite, watermelon tourmaline, aquamarine and amethyst at the centre.

Gold

If gemstones are the flowers of the mineral realm, gold on the other hand is certainly the noblest of metals. In 1981 Brazil became the world's third largest producer as new discoveries started to be worked. Malleability and sheer splendour make it unrivalled for the mounting of gemstones.

The metal is more often than not native to quartz veins or veins containing other minerals, such as sulphides, arsenides and tellurides. It is sometimes found scattered in iron ore, as in the Ouro Preto region, or in eluvium, as on the Diamantina plateau, or else in alluvium. Two underground mines located in this state: Morro Velho, near Belo Horizonte, and Passagem, near Mariana, are active.

Through superficial alteration, the veins release native gold which concentrates in the neighbouring eluvium and colluvium before enriching nearby alluvial stream deposits. The wealth of the alluvial deposits in the Minas Gerais iron-producing region is legendary, and was intensely exploited during the colonial period, when Brazil was the world's first producer of gold.

Rivers carry gold in the form of specks, flakes or nuggets. The nuggets are often rounded because of the metal's high degree of malleability. Alluvial deposits are plentiful in Brazil. In the states of Bahia, Goiás, Minas Gerais and Pará, gold rests on a gravel bed, covered by a layer of sterile sediments of varying thickness.

The most spectacular recent discovery was the Serra Pelada mine in Pará, where thousands of garimpeiros have already extracted millions of dollars worth of gold. Estimates of Brazil's reserves are being steadily revised upwards.

Gold nugget from the Carajás region, state of Pará, weighing 170 grammes, discovered in 1980.

Brazil

- DIAMOND
- EMERALD
- AQUAMARINE
- TOURMALINE
- RUBELLITE
- IMPERIAL TOPAZ
- BLUE TOPAZ
- CHRYSOBERYL
- OPAL
- KUNZITE
- BRAZILIANITE
- AMETHYST
- CITRINE
- QUARTZ
- AGATE
- GARNET
- OTHER STONES

RORAIMA

AMAZONAS

ACRE

RONDÔNIA

Glossary

Alluvial deposit: Debris and gems carried by a river; found along a riverbank.

Amorphous: Without form. Material that has no regular arrangement of atoms, hence no crystal structure.

Asterism: A term applied to the display of a rayed figure (star) by a gemstone usually when cut in cabochon.

Basal: Referring to planes or faces that form parallel to the base (bottom) of a crystal.

Cabochon: A facetless cutting style that produces convex surfaces.

Carat: Unit of weight equal to 200 mg.

Chatoyancy: Optical phenomenon displayed by certain gems that produce a thin bright light across a stone, most visible when cut in cabochon. Cat's-eye effect.

Cleavage: The property of a mineral whereby it is constrained to break along regular crystallographic planes (indicative of the internal crystal structure of the mineral).

Crystallization: The process whereby crystals are formed from a gaseous, liquid or molten state.

Density: Mass per unit volume.

Drusy: Surface encrusted with small projecting crystals.

Fluorescence: The emission of visible light by a gem when subjected to ultraviolet or X-radiation.

Gangue: The portion of an ore which is not economically valuable.

Geode: A small globular cavity found in some sedimentary rocks, normally partly filled by inward projecting crystals.

Hardness: Resistance a material offers to scratching or abrasion.

Inclusion: Internal landscape of a gemstone.

Interference: Effect produced of two or more light waves travelling the same path after travelling different distances.

Iridiscence: Light interference effect in thin films of gas or liquid, causing rainbow effects.

Kimberlite: The rock containing diamonds.

Metamorphism: Mineralogical and textural adjustments of solid rocks to changes in the physical and chemical environment.

Occurrence: The place where a mineral is found.

Pegmatite: Very coarse-grained granitic rock representing the last stages of crystallization of a magma. It is the primary source of most gemstones.

Pleochroism: Unequal absortion of the two portions of a doubly refracted beam of light producing two or more colours when observed through a dichroscope. It is the general term for dichroism and trichroism.

Refraction: The bending of light rays as they pass from one medium to another of different optical density at angles other than perpendicular to their boundary.

Refractive index: It is the ratio of the velocity of light in a vacuum to the velocity of light in the crystal. It is the optic density of the gemstone.

Specific gravity: The ratio of the weight of a substance to that of an equal volume of water at 4 degrees centigrade.

Translucent: Transmitting light, but diffusely.

Transparent: Transmitting light with a minimum of distortion.

Zoning: Systematic variation in the composition of a crystal, usually from core to outside edge.

Table of contents

Foreword 3

Introduction 5

Diamond 16

Emerald 20

Aquamarine 26

Other beryls 32

Tourmaline 36

Rubellite 47

Imperial topaz 56

Blue topaz 60

Chrysoberyl 64

Opal 68

Spodumene 72

Brazilianite 76

Amethyst 80

Citrine 88

Other quartzes 94

Chalcedony (agate) 102

Garnet 108

Collection stones 110

Corundums 124

Sculptures in gemmy material 126

Gold 130

Gem occurrences 132

Glossary 134

Printing and Binding
Grafica Riex Editora S.A.
Rua Silva Pinto, 9 - Vila Isabel
Tel. 208-0046 - Rio de Janeiro - RJ - Brazil